BRILLIANT BOBBY
& the Kids of Karma
the Wax Museum

Written by
Kevin Rakeen White

Illustrated by
Keith Williams

BRILLIANT BOBBY
& the kids of Karma
the Wax Museum

This book is dedicated to my sons and every other BRILLIANT BLACK BOY on the planet.

Written by
Kevin Rakeen White

Illustrated by
Keith Williams

"Rise and shine, Bobby!" Baba yelled as he pushed open my bedroom door. "I'm up, Baba. Just two more minutes and I'll be right there," I said, still half-asleep with my cover over my head. I was exhausted from the night before. I had to push myself extra hard just to make it to the bathroom. My father backtracked to my room to make sure that I was up and getting ready for school, but I made turtle progress, with the right side of my body hanging off the bed. Baba knows how much I dislike it when he opens my bedroom blinds to get me up, but it never seems to stop him.

"Bobby! Get up this very instant, young man," Baba said in his strong voice. "I want to see you downstairs for breakfast in fifteen minutes." With a face full of sunlight and not much energy, I rolled from my bed onto the floor. The floor always has a way of reminding me of who's boss, but I took a licking and kept on ticking, as Baba would say. The bathroom is one of my favorite places, where I can go and be myself without anyone saying anything about it. I love looking into the mirror, imagining that I am a great somebody!

"Today I am George Washington Carver!" I told myself as I looked into the mirror.

After my fifteen minutes were up, I could hear my father calling
my name from the bottom of the stairs. Needing more time,
I threw on my clothes and rushed downstairs half-dressed
and ready for school. With little to no time to eat, I grabbed
my lunch bag, toast, and a carton of orange juice. I gave my
mother a hug and a kiss. My father helped me get my belt on
and gave me a hug.
Off to the school bus I went, with a great big smile.

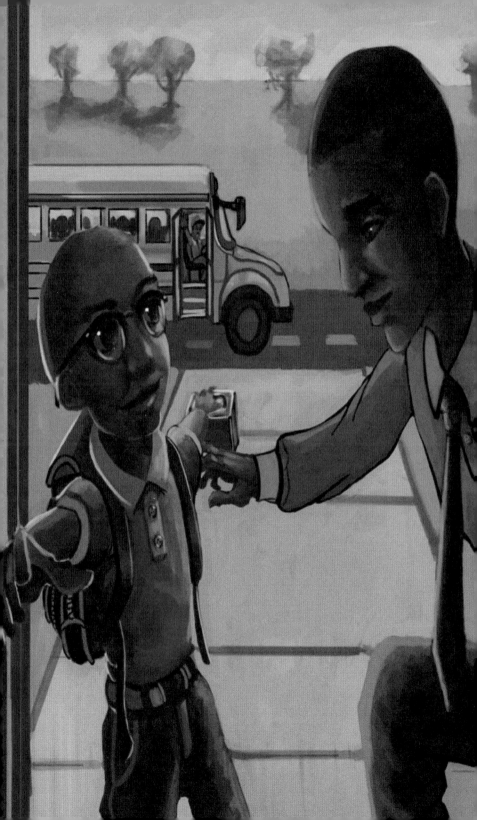

Today, everyone was a little more excited than usual, because we were going on a school trip to the Wax Museum. I was so excited that, when we arrived at school, I jumped from the top step of the bus. Before I could touch the ground, my glasses went crashing to the sidewalk. To make matters worse, I landed on top of them, breaking my glasses in three places. With my classmates laughing, I thought to myself, "Mama and Baba are going to kill me."

Militant Mike came over to help me get myself together. He placed his arm around me, saying, "Everything is going to be alright, Bobby. Let me see your frames. I can make them like new." Militant Mike smiled

Before we even reached the classroom, Militant Mike had already taped my glasses in three different places. "Here you go, Bobby. These are the new improved frames crafted by me, the militant one!" he exclaimed.

I have to say, they were just a little rocky from ear to ear. I didn't mind the tape too much, because I was able to see again. "Thanks, Militant Mike," I replied, adjusting my new frames. "They're not so bad after all."

As we headed through the school's doorway, some of the
students were laughing at my glasses, but Militant Mike jumped
right in for me. "Leave my man B alone! There's nothing wrong
with his frames. As a matter of fact, Bobby, you look brilliant
today." He smiled while looking at my glasses. "From this day on,
you will be Brilliant Bobby! If anyone has a problem with that,
and I do mean anyone, please come and see me." The students
were silent. They respected Mike.

Education, in the broadest of tru
will make an individual seek to he
regardless of race, regardless of
regardless of condition.

nse,
ople,
r

Once we reached the classroom, our teacher was waiting in the doorway to greet everyone. She smiled when she saw my glasses, saying, "New frames, I see. They are jaaaazzy!"

Militant Mike followed up with, "His new frames came with a new name, so you can call him Brilliant Bobby, Dr. Imani."

"I like that," she replied, nodding. That made me feel good. I liked Brilliant Bobby; it had a special ring to it. When everyone took their seats, Dr. Imani went over the schedule for the day. "First, it's morning affirmations, breakfast, and then we will board the bus for today's trip. Make sense?!"

"Makes sense!" the class responded in unison.

"Who wants to go first?" Dr. Imani asked.

"I am an educated warrior!" Sekou Bomani shouted.

"I am a beautiful African princess!" Zori exclaimed.

"I am the ancestors' promise of a better day!" Zion shouted.

"I am a great African warrior!" Aquae yelled, standing.

"I am an African prince!" Kevin shouted.

"I am a great dancer and fashion designer!" Tij shouted.

"I am a direct descendant of the Honorable Marcus Garvey, and a fierce African warrior scholar!" Militant Mike exclaimed.

"I am an amazing pianist!" Jahmere shouted.

"I am a reflection of God's most prized possession!" Saida Mirmbe said.

"I am Imhotep's legacy, reflecting his divine light as a great physician!" Zaccai Ibekwe proclaimed.

"I am a royal king!" Ade-Oba shouted.

"I am an eloquent and renowned poet, reflecting Maya Angelou's brilliance!" Laila Imani exclaimed.

"I am an agricultural genius, caring for the land and safety!" I shouted.

"And I am a master teacher with a class full of wonderful students!" concluded Dr. Imani, in her sweet and powerful voice.

After our morning affirmations and breakfast, we boarded the bus right on schedule. That's one of the many reasons why I love Dr. Imani— when she says something is to be, it will be. I was able to get my window seat, just like I prayed for the night before. During the ride, I imagined what it must have been like for George Washington Carver as a child, a young boy, and a man. I started to daydream. Before I knew it, we were pulling up to the museum. A strong feeling came over me as I exited the bus.

In awe, we stood in front of the museum, which looked like a creation straight out of the Mali Empire. It looked like a huge sand castle, with spikes protruding from it. The front door stood about three stories tall, with a large ankh dead center as a door knob. The windows were framed in gold. The building itself took up two city blocks. As we approached the entrance, faces and historical events jumped out at us from the engravings that seemed to be in rhythm with a tune that only Fela could capture.

Entering the museum was like stepping off an airplane in Africa
for the first time. The energy was vibrating, reflecting faces and
moments from times past. We were greeted by a beautiful
woman dressed in traditional African garb, and the men were
very muscular, with matching African garb. Of all the stories
that I'd heard about this place, none of them did it justice. The
first thing we heard as we entered the museum was, "Welcome
home."

Dr. Imani had a tour set up for us by one of the staff members. There were some things she wanted us to get as a class, for the projects that we had to turn in at the end of the marking period. After the tour, she allowed moments of freedom. We really liked that part of the tour. I was exploring the slave quarters of the ship, reading about the children who were chained and shackled in what was called "the belly of the beast." I cried before I left that area of the museum. Reading about people my age and younger who had been treated so badly made me feel like I should be doing something so that would never happen again, but what?

No one really knew what Militant Mike was thinking. We just knew it was something strong. He stayed in the "belly of the beast," reading and taking pictures during our free time. I'm not sure if I was the only who caught a tear fall from his right eye, but he knew that I knew. He gave me a nod, and I understood him without words. It was a moment between friends, and no one else.

I spent part of my free time roaming the building, thinking of all the great achievers the museum introduced to us. Proud and filled with new life and energy, I stumbled into a farming exhibit and found myself standing face to knee with the man himself, George Washington Carver. G-pop's father told us many stories about Elder-Ancestor Carver. He was one of the greatest to have stepped foot onto a farm. G-pop's father told us that Elder-Ancestor Carver could hear the plants talk to him.

Elder-Ancestor Carver towered over me like the Empire State Building towers over taxicabs during rush hour. Even though he was a wax figure, his was still a strong African-American face so full of light, life, and love. Elder-Ancestor Carver, a real model who I will always remember. I had to take a few steps back just to get a full view of his greatness. This was my moment with Elder-Ancestor Carver. I smiled, then took out my notebook and pencil to leave a note under his foot.

One day, I will add something very important to world, just like Elder-Ancestor Carver did for us. My G-pop's father introduced me to his works, and really likes him a lot. He said that Elder-Ancestor Carver is his hero, and the reason why he became a botanist. I love my G-pop's father. He's the reason I also love plants and the outdoors. I think I will also become a botanist, since my grandfather is my hero.

The wax figure looked so real, it was almost scary. As Dr. Imani would say, there was a lot of our story in there. I really liked this place. Mama always says that time flies when you're having fun or enjoying yourself. She was right. It seemed like we had just arrived, and then it was time to depart.

On our way back to the school, Militant Mike and I were sitting together in silence. It was weird not talking the whole way back. I think we were still in the museum, thinking about the children who we were reading about. I wanted to know what was in Militant Mike's head, but the time was far from being right, so I just kept to myself.

When we got back to the school, it was time for us to be picked up. The day was amazing. I love learning about history. Even though the morning was a bit rocky, I made it through, and the rest of the day was great.

At the end of the day, I ran over to Dr. Imani and said, "Thanks for loving us enough to know that our history is important to us. I now know without doubt what I want to be when I grow up." I smiled from ear to ear.

"What's that, my young sir?" replied Dr. Imani, with a huge smile on her face.

"I want to be a botanist and a historian. I want to help cultivate the land and tell stories about our people," I told her excitedly.

Dr. Imani just smiled and said, "You can be whatever you want to be, Brilliant Bobby."

We smiled together as tears of joy streamed from her eyes.

"Okay, Dr. Imani, my Baba is here. See you tomorrow!" I yelled while running to my father's open arms. I couldn't wait to tell Mama and Baba about the adventure I had.

I AM...

Name: Bobby Sims

Nickname: Brilliant Bobby

Spirit: George Washington Carver

Age: 9

Race: African American

Grade: 5th

Dreams: To be one of the world's most powerful botanist and historians.

Hobbies: Reading, writing, traveling, watching sci-fi movies, science, and listing to classical music.

Skill: Visionary

Diet: Vegetarian

Family: Mother and father, grandparents on both sides, great grandparents on his mother's side, uncle's name is Bobby

Signature: Glasses taped in three places

INTRODUCUE YOURSELF

Name:

Nickname:

Spirit:

Age:

Race:

Grade:

Dreams:

Hobbies:

Skill:

Diet:

Family:

Signature:

Your photo here

ABOUT THE SPIRIT OF BRILLIANT BOBBY

George Washington Carver was born into slavery in Diamond, Missouri, around 1864. The exact year and date of his birth are unknown. Carver went on to become one of the most prominent scientists and inventors of his time, as well as a teacher at the Tuskegee Institute. Carver devised more than one hundred products using one of these crops—the peanut—including dyes, plastics, and gasoline. He died in 1943.

Lesson at a Glance:

Summary: During a field trip with his class, Bobby experienced an emotional journey, with feelings of both sadness and joy. He is reminded of his ancestors' painful past, while learning about great achievers such as George Washington Carver. He is inspired to one day become a historian, so that he can educate himself, as well as others.

Skills:

- Comprehension Skill: Note Details
- Vocabulary: *affirmation, botany, brilliant, improved, plantation, vegetarian, visionary, wondrous, historian*
- Comprehension Strategy: Make Connections
- Language Focus: Nouns
- Literary Focus: Character
- Fluency: Expression

Before Reading

Building Background – Access Prior Knowledge:
Display the cover and read the title. Explain that The Wax Museum is the first of many books about a 9-year-old boy named Bobby who loves learning about the history of his people. Have students share what they know about their history. Ask: "What might a boy called Brilliant Bobby like to do for fun?"

Set a Purpose
Have them read pg. 28 "I AM...". Then help them set a purpose for reading, such as: "I will read to find out how Bobby Sims got the nickname Brilliant Bobby."

More Pre-Reading Activities
Comprehension Skill – Note Details: Preview the comprehension skill by having students explain what is happening on page 2. Bobby's father wakes him up, Bobby tries to convince him that he just needs two more seconds, and his father backtracks to see if he is up.
Have students turn to pages 3-4. Say: "Details are important pieces of information that help you visualize and understand a story's setting, characters, and events."
Explain how the author uses details to clarify Bobby's reluctance to get out of bed, and why the bathroom is one of Bobby's favorite places.

Vocabulary:
Introduce the vocabulary words using index cards, chart paper, or any other type of visual aid. Have students identify words they already know. Then discuss the words and their meanings. Ask questions such as the following, and have students explain their reasoning:

Which of the following is a positive affirmation?
"I can do anything I put my mind to," or "I may as well give up; these math problems are too difficult for me?"

Which is related to botany?
The meteorologist who tells us the weather, or the branch of biology that deals with plant life?

Which of the two is a brilliant idea?
Doing your homework as soon as you come home from school, or waiting until moments before you have to go to bed?

What would you consider new?
A typewriter or a laptop?

What would be the ideal lunch for a vegetarian? Hamburgers and French fries, or a garden salad?

During Reading

Read the Story. Distribute the "Read the Story" worksheet. Review the directions and questions. Then have students read Brilliant Bobby. They might read the story independently. Or guide the reading, using these prompts.

Do you think that Militant Mike is a good friend?
Why or why not?

Why do you think Bobby's classmates respected Militant Mike?

Why do you think Dr. Imani liked the nickname Brilliant Bobby?

How would you explain the purpose of morning affirmations in Dr. Imani's classroom?

More During Reading Activities

Comprehension Strategy Mini Lesson – Making Connections: Explain the comprehension strategy, telling students that active readers make the following connections as they read: T-S, T-T, and T-W.

Text-to-self (T-S):
What does this remind me of in my life?
What is this similar to in my life?
How is this different from my life?
Has something like this ever happened to me?
How does this relate to my life?
What were my feelings when I read this?

Text-to-text (T-T):
What does this remind me of in another book I've read?
How is this text similar to other things I've read?
How is this different from other books I've read?
Have I read about something like this before?

Text-to-world (T-W):
What does this remind me of in the real world?
How is this text similar to things that happen in the real world?
How is this different from things that happen in the real world?
How did that part relate to the world around me?

Read aloud page 2. Model the strategy. Say: "When I read this page, I think about how I'm not always ready to get out of bed when my alarm goes off in the morning. Like Bobby, I don't have too much energy until I feel water on my face in the morning. This helps me visualize how sleepy Bobby was when his dad woke him up. I think about how he says he rolled from his bed onto the floor. As I read that line, I create a picture in my head of him falling to the floor."

As you guide the reading, pause for students to make connections.

Language Focus Mini Lesson - Nouns: Direct attention to the word bus and the word buses. Write the words on the board.
Say: "A noun names a person, a place, or a thing." Point to the noun bus. Reinforce the concept: "The word bus is a noun that names one thing. It is also a singular noun."
Point to the word buses. Say: "A noun can also name more than one thing. The noun buses names more than one bus. It is a plural noun."
Tell students that a plural noun is often formed by adding -s to the end of the noun. Say: "For nouns that end in ch, sh, s, x, or z, add -es to form the plural. For nouns that end in a consonant and a y, change the y to and i and add -es."
Distribute worksheet titled "One or More?" Ask students to look for singular and plural nouns as they reread the story.

ELL: English-Language Learners - Language Transfer
Plural nouns may present challenges for native speakers of languages that have no plural forms for nouns, such as Chinese, Hmong, Korean, and Vietnamese. Students may say "They saw bus" instead of "They saw buses." Help students practice using plural nouns by correctly restating sentences and emphasizing the plural noun: "When they looked out of the window, they saw two buses."

Talk About It: Have students share their answers to the "Think About It" questions in the back of the book.
Answers:
1. Answers will vary. Have the students support their opinions.
2. Answers will vary. Have the students support their opinions.
3. Sample answer: Bobby will tell his parents how much he learned at the Wax Museum.
4. Sample answer: So that others will be informed.
5. Answers will vary. Have the students support their opinions.
6. Answers will vary. Have the students support their opinions.
7. Sample answer: Excited, because learning takes place somewhere other than the classroom.

After Reading

Literary Focus – Character: Tell the students that characters are the people in a story.

Say: "One way to better understand and enjoy a story is to understand its characters. Readers can learn a lot about the characters by paying attention to what the characters say and do."

Call on a volunteer to read aloud page 16. Ask: "What do you learn about Militant Mike from his time spent in the 'belly of the beast' and his reaction to being there? How is his reaction the same or different from Bobby's?"

Remind students that they soon learn that Militant Mike wasn't the only character to have an emotional reaction to what he saw at the Wax Museum. Say: "Knowing that Dr. Imani had tears streaming down her cheeks helps you better understand that this was an emotional journey taken via the Wax Museum."

Comprehension – Note Details
Distribute worksheet titled "Story Details." Have students work with partners to write down important details from different parts of the story.

Vocabulary: Have students create sentences or fictional stories using the vocabulary words from the story.

Fluency – Expression: Tell students that when they read with expression, they use their voices to make the dialogue sound as if the characters are really speaking. Read page 2 with expression to model for students. Have students work in pairs and take turns reading dialogue from the story.

Writing: Possible writing prompts:
Have students write how they'd feel if they took the same trip Bobby and his classmates took to the Wax Museum. How would they generate a plan so that history doesn't repeat itself?

Explain why you think Dr. Imani makes the students say morning affirmations.

Talk About It:
Why is it important for children to learn about their history?

Why were Brilliant Bobby and Militant Mike crying during their trip to the museum?

What do you think Brilliant Bobby will tell his parents when he gets home?
- Why is it important to share the history that you learn?
- What is your opinion of Bobby's friend, Militant Mike?
- How is Bobby's at-home morning routine connected to what you do in the morning?
- How do you feel when you go on class trips? Why?

Glossary of Terms

Affirmation - Positively stating or asserting something

Botany - The science of plants; the branch of biology that deals with plant
life

Brilliant - Extremely intelligent

Historian - An expert in history

Improved - To bring into a more desirable or excellent condition

Plantation - Usually a large farm or estate on which cotton, tobacco, or
coffee is cultivated

Vegetarian - A person who does not eat meat

Visionary - Purely idealistic or speculative

Wondrous - Wonderful; remarkable

Aligned to the following Common Core Standards...
(www.pdesas.org)

1.1.3.D: Demonstrate comprehension/understanding before reading, during reading, and after reading on grade level texts through strategies such as retelling, summarizing, note taking, connecting to prior knowledge, supporting assertions about text with evidence from text, and non-linguistic representations.

R3.A.1.1: Identify and interpret the meaning of vocabulary.

R3.A.1.3: Make inferences and draw conclusions based on text.

R3.A.1.4.1: Identify and/or explain stated or implied main ideas and relevant supporting details from text. Note: items may target specific paragraphs. Items might ask about information in the text that is most important or helpful for understanding a particular fact or idea. Items may require recalling key information stated in text.

CC.1.1.3.E: Read with accuracy and fluency to support comprehension: Read on-Level text with purpose and understanding. Read on-level text orally with accuracy, appropriate rate, and expression on successive readings. Use context to confirm or self-correct word recognition and understanding, rereading as necessary.

E03.B-K.1.1.1: Answer questions to demonstrate understanding of a text, referring explicitly to the text as the basis for the answers.

E03.B-K.1.1.2: Determine the main idea of a text; recount the key details and explain how they support the main idea.

Name

Read the Story
Read the assigned page(s). Answer the assigned question(s).

1. What do you learn about Bobby from what he says to himself in the bathroom mirror?

2. Based on what Bobby does before leaving for school, how do you think he feels about his parents?

3. How did Bobby get the nickname Brilliant Bobby?

4. How does a person feel when you are a person of your word? Explain why.

5. What was the significance of the time Bobby spent with Elder-Ancestor Carver?

Name

Story Details:
Details are important pieces of information that help you visualize and understand a story's setting, characters, and events.

Write the important details that help you visualize the setting, characters, and events from The Wax Museum.

Bobby's morning routine (pages 2-5)

Militant Mike (pages 10-14)

Bobby's trip to the Wax Museum (pages 19-23)

Name

One or More?
A singular noun names one person, place or thing. A plural noun names two or more people, places, or things. Plural nouns often end with -s or -es.

Singular Nouns	friend	teacher	bus	story
Plural Nouns	friends	teachers	buses	stories

Look through The Wax Museum to find singular and plural nouns. Write at least ten singular nouns and ten plural nouns.

Singular Nouns	Plural Nouns

PLACES IN OUR COMMUNITY

Sankofa Freedom Academy is the community charter school that we attend. It is a K-12 school that is supported by the families and businesses in the community.

Freedom Market is the community SUPER mega food market that is owned and run by the community members.

Akoben Martial Arts Center house classes, workshops, and national conferences in the areas of self defense, health and wellness.

Cuttin' Up is the community barbershop where some of our older brothers, uncles, fathers, and friends work.

Cuttin' Up Too is the saloon in the community where some of our sisters, mothers, aunties, cousins, and friends work.

New Media Technology Studio is an ever evolving multimillion dollar media studio that house the community movie theater, music recording studio, community tv & radio station, and a 6 weeks summer enrichment program for all who wants to attend. They offer master classes for children, adults, and elders.

Imani University is one of many universities that's in our surrounding area. It is also the first choice for a large number of graduates from our school.

Harambee Trade Group is the leading trade school in the country. Our graduates have many choices to pick from when it comes to furthering their gifts and talents. "You name a trade and we'll help you master it", is their slogan.

Umoja Circle is the community playground

Nia Clothing Shop & Cleaners is the place to get the latest fashions, from new age hip-hop wear to cultural attire of your choosing. If you're looking to get new for now or through back for a 60's, 70's, 80's, or 90's party this is the place to be. If you're looking to be made by taylor, just
take your threads to back of the shop and get laid.

Black Panther's Protection Inc. Community police station
We have a number of other businesses in in our community that i'll share with you later in the
story, as for now, you can share with us the makeup of your community.

Cuttin' Up Too

Harambee Trade Group

New Media Technology Studio

Cuttin' Up

Akoben Martial Arts Center

Black Panther's Protection Inc.

Nia Clothing Shop & Cleaners

Sankofa Freedom Academy

Freedom Market

Umoja Circle

Imani University

Made in the USA
Las Vegas, NV
27 April 2024

89228105R00033